KEYS TO OPTIMAL MENTAL HEALTH

God bless you,

Magna Porterfield

KEYS TO OPTIMAL
MENTAL HEALTH

Magna Parks-Porterfield, Ph.D.

Copyright © 2015 Magna Parks-Porterfield, Ph.D.
All rights reserved.

ISBN: 1522810455
ISBN 13: 9781522810452
Library of Congress Control Number: 2015921163
CreateSpace Independent Publishing Platform
North Charleston, South Carolina

ACKNOWLEDGEMENTS

I would like to first thank my husband, Ron Porterfield, who gave me the idea to write this book, supported me throughout the whole process, and carefully critiqued my work. I also am grateful to Shelley Quinn for strongly encouraging me to write and for James Hoffer who edited the manuscript. In addition, I would like to thank Phil Mills, M.D., Edwin Noyes, M.D. and Lewis Walton, Esq. for reviewing my work and providing helpful feedback.

Finally, and most important, I thank God for giving me the strength and tools for sharing this information with others.

CONTENTS

	Acknowledgements	v
	Introduction	ix
Chapter 1	The Foundation–Change Your Lifestyle	1
Chapter 2	You Are What You Think	12
Chapter 3	Develop Self-Control	16
Chapter 4	Grow From Adversity	21
Chapter 5	Develop A Healthy Conscience	29
Chapter 6	Focus Less on Self and More On Others	36
Chapter 7	Cultivate Lasting Happiness	41
Chapter 8	Develop An Active Religious Life	46
Chapter 9	A Brief Summary	53
	Endnotes	55

INTRODUCTION

Mental health—When we hear this phrase, we typically think of conditions such as depression, anxiety, stress, and other psychological concerns. But, over a half century ago the World Health Organization indicated that health is more than the absence of disease or infirmity. It involves having a complete state of physical, mental, and social well-being. And as a psychologist, I am particularly interested in helping others attain that complete state of *mental* well-being and health.

It is because of this that I decided to write this book. Over the years, those in the field of psychology have become increasingly interested in looking at how people can achieve optimal mental health, and this includes both those who have been diagnosed with a psychological disorder as well as those who have not.

The research in this area has yielded a wealth of practical information to help achieve this goal. However, thousands of years before scientists studied this, some wonderful principles were given to us in an ancient book called the Bible—which I consider the **master** psychology textbook.

The principles for mental health presented in this book have been gleaned from both science and the Bible. It is my hope that those who read this information will understand more about their mental well-being and will realize that it is within their power to make changes to achieve optimal mental health.

Magna Parks-Porterfield, Ph.D.
Seale, Alabama
December 2014

CHAPTER 1

THE FOUNDATION-CHANGE YOUR LIFESTYLE

When I was obtaining my doctorate in psychology, there was not one class offered on understanding how the way we take care of our bodies—through common sense health practices such as diet, exercise, and sleep—affects our mental health. I am not sure that much has changed in graduate training in psychology over the past 20-plus years. However, over the last decade or more, there has been increasing evidence to show the relationship between lifestyle and mental health.

Interestingly, there is even research that shows that lifestyle choices can also help those who suffer from some of the most common psychological disorders—such as depression, anxiety, and other mental health difficulties.

In a review of studies, for example, Dr. Roger Walsh found that lifestyle factors—which he terms "therapeutic lifestyle changes"—are sometimes as effective as drugs or psychotherapy in treating various mental health concerns.[1] This was exciting news for me, because for the past eight or more years I have encouraged my clients to make lifestyle changes as a means of improving their mental health and overall well-being. The results have been phenomenal! Those who made these changes experienced less sadness, reduced nervousness, more clearness in thinking, increased ability to control emotions and many other mental health benefits.

What are some of these lifestyle factors? Let us consider a few significant ones.

NUTRITION

Over 100 years ago a health educator stated that "It cannot be too often repeated that whatever is taken into the stomach affects not only the body but ultimately the mind as well."[2] If you desire optimal mental heath, one of the first steps you must take is to make sure you are eating healthy foods that will feed your mind—specifically, your brain. It has been stated that at least 50 per cent of what we eat goes to our brain. Surely the brain can be considered a greedy organ! Given this fact, it is important that we take in those foods that we know will help the brain.

One of the best foods that contribute to optimal mental health are plant-based foods—namely, fruits, grains, legumes, nuts, and vegetables. These foods contain a variety of nutrients that are important for our brains to function more effectively, such as B vitamins, essential fatty acids, healthy carbohydrates, and various phytochemicals.

But we must also avoid foods and substances that can impair our mental functioning, such as caffeine and sugar (especially table sugar). Although the research on caffeine is mixed, I believe that caffeine is a drug that enhances some mental abilities in the short term, but in the long term has far-reaching negative effects on the mind. And with regards to sugar, it is advisable to minimize the use of white, processed table sugar and moderately use sugars that are less processed, such as honey and maple syrup. There is evidence to suggest that using a lot of sugar can have a negative impact on mental health.[3,4]

This information does not at all cover all that can be said about diet and mental health. However, if what was mentioned above is followed, I believe that it will give you a "jump start" in helping your mind function more effectively.

Thus far we've only considered *what* we eat as it relates to our mental health. However, there is another part of nutrition that is just as important—the timing of our meals. It has been stated that, "our health isn't just about what we eat, but when we eat"[5] If we eat at all times of the day, and do not incorporate the principle of regularity—order and consistency—this disrupts our body's circadian rhythm. This is the "clock" in our bodies that directs the various activities we engage in such as sleeping, working, and eating. In order for this not to happen, we should refrain from erratic eating, such as not eating on a schedule and/or eating between meals. In this way we can keep our circadian rhythms working properly, which will in turn help our minds to function effectively. As one author says, "Regularity in eating is very important for health of body and serenity of mind"[6]

In my work as a psychologist, I have seen the positive results that can occur when a decision is made to practice many of the dietary principles mentioned above. Several of my clients have reported that they experienced more alertness, better mood, enhanced concentration, and other mental health benefits when they changed their diet and became more regular with their eating schedules. As a result, it has become my practice to routinely focus on this with clients, no matter their initial concerns. This lifestyle change is critical and should always be considered in the quest for optimal mental health.

REST

Another lifestyle factor that contributes to optimal mental health is adequate rest or sleep. Unfortunately, it is a well-known fact that most people are sleep-deprived. Sadly, this lack of sleep does have an affect on our health, including our mental health. It has been found that when we don't get enough sleep it can slow down thought processes, impair memory, make learning difficult, alter mood, and cause irritability and anger.[7] It cannot be overstated that getting a good night's rest is essential for optimal mental health.

You may now be asking, How much sleep do I need? It is generally agreed that adults need approximately seven to eight hours of sleep. Of course, for growing children and adolescents the sleep requirement is more (at least one to two hours). And as with nutrition, regularity is also essential. In order for us to benefit the most from our time of rest at night, we must have routine times for going to bed and for awakening each morning.

The timing for this routine is also proven to be important. Research shows that there are critical processes in our brains that begin before midnight during sleep. One of these is the peak production of melatonin, which helps us get more quality sleep. Based on the repair work that goes on, it would be best to be asleep by 10 p.m. These hours before midnight are critical for us to get the most benefits from our rest. In fact, it has been stated that "two hours' good sleep before twelve o'clock is worth more than four hours after twelve o'clock."[8] What this tells us is that it's not only how much sleep we get, but when we go to sleep that is important.

EXERCISE

Have you ever felt a little down and decided to go outside and take a walk? Did you feel your mood lift after doing so? This may not always happen for everyone, but I am sure that many reading this can relate to this experience. Exercise does wonders for our mental health! In fact exercise releases various chemicals that make our bodies feel good. You've probably heard of some of these chemicals such as endorphins and serotonin. When these are released in our bodies, we experience wonderful results such as enhanced mood, reduced anxiety, clearer thinking, and a greater sense of well-being.

Another benefit of exercise as related to mental health is that it increases our resilience, which is the ability to bounce back after adversity. It is has been shown that those who exercise regularly have increased stamina to withstand stress. So when they are faced with challenging circumstances and situations, those individuals who exercise are better able to cope with whatever comes their way. I can personally attest to this. Several years ago, my first husband died suddenly. This was a quite difficult time of life for me. I was on a walking program prior to his death. But after he died, I increased the regularity of my exercise. This helped me cope more effectively with this sudden loss and also helped me during the grieving process.

One final important note regarding exercise is that it tends to be more beneficial when it is done outdoors. In a review of studies that compared natural environments (such as a park) to artificial environments (such as a gym), researchers found that those exposed to the natural environments experienced positive changes, such as decreased anger, anxiety, fatigue, and sadness.[9] When we exercise outside, we are exposed to more fresh air and sunlight, both of which are quite beneficial for our minds.

So, I encourage you to get active and exercise, especially out doors, and you will be that much closer to achieving optimal mental health!

OTHER LIFESTYLE FACTORS:

In addition to having a proper diet, getting adequate sleep and exercising, there are other lifestyle activities that we can do to have optimal mental health. These include the following:

- Drink adequate water. The brain is made up largely of water. Thus, it helps to regularly replenish our bodies and brains with this inexpensive, refreshing drink! How much water should you drink? Some say eight ounces a day, while others say half your body weight in ounces. Whatever formula you choose, just make sure that your urine is typically pale in

color (unless you eat something like asparagus or vitamin supplements that sometimes make urine more yellowish in color).
- Get adequate sunlight. Exposure to sunlight helps with the production of vitamin D and serotonin (a brain chemical that helps regulate our mood), both of which affect our mental functioning.
- Get fresh air. Spending time outdoors for exercise and sun also allows us to get fresh air, which is quite beneficial for our minds. Fresh air, especially that which is close to nature and which we get right after a thunderstorm, provides negative ions which have been found to be quite helpful for mental and physical health. It is also important to get adequate air by learning how to breathe properly.

It is my strong belief that implementing lifestyle factors provides a foundation for optimal mental health. Before we can truly benefit from the remaining principles presented in this book, the groundwork must be laid by doing whatever we can to build healthy bodies and brains. This can happen as we apply these lifestyle principles to the best of our ability. It does take much work and effort to make these changes, but if you persevere, you will see the wonderful results!

PRACTICAL APPLICATION:

1. Review your diet. One easy way to do this may be to chart what you eat (and when you eat) for the next three or four days.
2. If you find that you are not eating at least five servings of fruits and vegetables every day, gradually add these foods to your diet. Also, eat more whole grains, legumes, and a moderate amount of nuts each day. Work on reducing or removing unhealthy products such as white sugar and replacing them with healthy substitutes (such as fruit-sweetened items). Try to stay away from snacking between meals and eating after 6:30 each night.
3. Start incorporating more exercise into your life. You may begin with walking at least 10 minutes a day and gradually increasing that over time. Spend less time in front of the television and even the computer (other than when you have to use the latter for work).
4. Work on getting to bed by no later than 10 p.m. This may be challenging for many who

are used to staying up late. But, if you resolve to change this and re-arrange your activities, it is possible. Try to develop a regular sleeping and waking time each day.
5. Get at least 15 to 20 minutes of sunlight each day (more if you have darker skin).
6. Drink at least 8 eight ounce glasses of water a day. You can start this by drinking two glasses of water as soon as you wake up each day and no closer than a half hour before you eat breakfast.
7. Get outdoors as often as you can and try to go to nature spots frequently, such as the park, the mountains, or a waterfall.

CHAPTER 2

YOU ARE WHAT YOU THINK

"For as he thinketh in his heart so is he." This was written in the book of Proverbs by the wise king Solomon nearly 3,000 years ago and it is ever so true! Our thoughts often determine who we are, which includes what we do, how we feel, and even what we say. Psychologists honed in on this principle about 50 years ago. Now scientific evidence reveals that changing our thoughts can contribute to our mental health and is even helpful for various psychological concerns including depression, anxiety, stress, and others.

One of the main concepts we need to understand regarding the impact of our thoughts is that of "self-talk"—that is, what we tell ourselves. If we were to pay close attention to our self-talk, we would be amazed at what we would discover. Some of us, for example, are constantly putting ourselves down or criticizing ourselves for mistakes, which can lead to poor self-worth and other related problems. Others are quick to think negatively about people or situations, which leads to problems with sad mood, irritability, or even clinical depression. On the other hand, some learn how to experience peace, joy and contentment by telling themselves things that are encouraging and uplifting, no matter their life circumstances. So, as you can see, it is possible to actually enhance or impair your mental and emotional state by changing your self-talk.

As we work on changing our thoughts, it doesn't take long to recognize that we have to unlearn something that we've been taught from a very young age. This is the belief that other things, people or circumstances dictate how we feel, act or what we say. Statements such as "He made me feel _____" or "She caused me to do_____" are not true. No one or thing can make us do anything. We are given the power of choice to decide how we will talk, think, or act. And when we truly grasp this concept, it can release us from the bondage of being controlled by people or circumstances. Whenever this principle is remembered and put into practice, it can help us cope with difficulties in a more effective manner.

It is important to add that we must also do our part to strengthen healthy thoughts by feeding our minds with good "food." Specifically, it is critical that we are careful about what we read, listen to, and watch. If we are exposing ourselves to material that is not uplifting, such as entertainment TV, movies, books, and music—these will impair how we think. However, if we listen to inspiring music or watch and read things that will enrich us, our thoughts will be more wholesome. So, monitoring these activities can provide an environment where healthy thoughts will flourish and grow.

It has been said that, "we need to place a high value upon the right control of our thoughts."[10] When we consider the impact that our thoughts have on our lives, and in particular, our mental health, this statement makes perfect sense. We must make a conscious effort to only think that which will uplift, empower, and encourage us. This is one of the reasons that the Bible writer Paul tells that whatever is true, honest, just, and pure we should make it a practice to "think on these things" (Philippians 4:8).

Are you willing to make a commitment today to develop healthy thinking? If you do, you will not regret it. And, as stated by one expert, you will "often experience lasting changes in your mood, outlook, and productivity."[11] This will not be an easy process, but with patience, time, and much effort it can be done. Then you will be on the road to obtaining optimal mental health!

PRACTICAL APPLICATION

1. Spend three or four days writing down the thoughts that you have.
2. If you notice a pattern of unhealthy thoughts, write down thoughts that counteract them. For example, if you are prone to say to yourself, "This is going to be rotten day," you can change that to "Even though things are not looking very good, the circumstances of this day do not have to dictate how I feel or think."
3. Practice replacing your unhealthy thoughts with inspirational passages from the Bible. Write these passages on cards and review them throughout the day.
4. Monitor the music you listen to, the books you read, the movies and TV programs you watch. Make an effort to remove those activities that will not help you to have healthy thoughts and replace them with wholesome ones.

CHAPTER 3

DEVELOP SELF-CONTROL

WHO WOULD THINK that self-control has anything to do with mental health? But, it does! Self-control is important for regulating our desires, words, thoughts, and other activities. This can be challenging because in our world today we are encouraged to obtain instant gratification. We are also strongly influenced to do or say what we want whenever we want, with few to no restrictions. So, the concept of controlling one's self—which often involves self-denial—can seem restrictive and even boring to many. However, for optimal mental health, self-control is crucial.

In the 1960s Dr. Walter Mischel conducted an experiment that helped us better understand the impact of exercising self-control from a young age. In this study, known as the Marshmallow Test, Dr. Mischel presented children with a treat, one of which was a marshmallow, and gave them two options: eat the treat immediately or wait in the room alone until the researcher returned, at which time they could get two treats. Dr. Mischel followed the lives of these children for years after the original experiment. What he found was that those who waited to eat the treat were healthier and happier, did better in school, earned more money, were less likely to use drugs, spent less time in jail, and had other positive outcomes in life.

In the Bible we find some insightful information about self-control. For example, Proverbs 25:28 states that "he that hath no rule over his own spirit is like a city that is broken down, and without walls." Many ancient cities had walls that were built around them for protection. Without such walls the individuals within were open to attacks from their enemies. When we do not have "rule over" or control our "spirit"—which refers to our emotions, passions, or desires—we are similar to a city with broken walls. We will act or speak, for example, without much thought. Or, we may have problems with managing anger, giving in to inappropriate sexual desires, overeating, or making impulsive decisions, which leave us in a weak, defenseless mental state.

Another thing to consider with self-control is that when we continually give in to unhealthy desires, habits, or emotions, we can become enslaved to them. For example, you may spend several hours a day watching entertainment television or movies every evening after work. You may recognize that this takes up a lot of your time, but you are so drawn to the TV or movies that it becomes difficult for you to stop watching them. What is actually happening is that this habit becomes one that rules your life, similar to a slave master ruling his servant. However, if you make the decision to watch only one hour or less of entertainment television (or even better, none at all!) you become your own "master" so to speak and you're no longer enslaved by this habit.

As you exert more control in your life, this results in a stronger brain/mind, which contributes to optimal mental health.

With all this said, we all are aware from experience that exercising self-control is much more easily said than done. Consider the words of the Bible writer Paul:

"And every man that striveth for the mastery is temperate in all things.... I therefore so run, not as uncertainly; so fight I, not as one that beateth the air: But I keep under my body, and bring it into subjection" (1 Corinthians 9:25-27).

The words "temperate" and keeping "under" the body to "bring it into subjection" reveal that controlling one's self requires effort and discipline. And, to be honest, this can be hard and even painful work! But to be successful with this, it is important to make a conscious decision to press forward—denying self, delaying gratification, etc.— because the outcome will be rewarding not only mentally, but physically and spiritually as well.

PRACTICAL APPLICATION:

In the book *Willpower* by Dr. Roy Baumeister, he shares many strategies, based on research, that can help with self-control. Here are a few of them (in an adapted version):

1. Learn how to distract yourself from your own desires and difficulties. For example, if you're tempted to overeat, develop a strategy that will divert your mind (such as calling a friend or taking a walk outside) from that temptation.

2. Make resolutions in front of another person. This provides some accountability.
3. Anticipate the situations where you are more likely to lose self-control and make plans to deal with such situations.
4. Set up clear rules in the areas where you are weak. For example, you can determine that you will not allow yourself to hang out with certain friends because this encourages you to engage in a certain behavior or to think in a certain way that is not healthy.
5. Become more consistent with religious activities. Research shows that religious people have more self-control and are more successful in building power to resist unhealthy desires, temptations, and the like.[12]

CHAPTER 4

GROW FROM ADVERSITY

Many of us have been exposed to very difficult and trying experiences in our lives, including traumatic childhoods, painful marriages, loss of a loved one, and health challenges. Coping with these circumstances can be very hard and can also take a toll both psychologically and physically. As a psychologist, I was taught that one of the ways to deal with such experiences is to spend time talking about it and seeking to gain insight as a means of emotional healing.

It is true that there can be some relief gained from understanding the impact of past (and even recent) painful events in our lives. However, I now believe that spending too much time on these experiences can actually get in the way of our healing, emotionally and mentally.

With this in mind, I would like to suggest that another key to optimal mental health is to "move past our past." I am sure there are some who are now asking, "Is it possible to really do that?" Well, the answer is yes. And one of the ways to do so is to look at how difficult experiences can make you (or has made you) a better person.

Over the last 20 or so years, psychologists have looked at a concept known as "post-traumatic growth." This is defined as positive psychological change experienced as a result of the struggle with highly challenging circumstances. Notice that this definition reveals that growth after a trauma involves a "struggle." It is important to keep this in mind because the process of growing after traumatic experiences is not one that is quick or easy. It is very likely that you will experience distress, pain, fear, and other negative emotions as you face various challenges in life. These feelings can occur along with growth. But as you emerge from the difficulties that you encounter, you can become a stronger person with a more determined focus and an overall better outlook on life.

How does one grow after adversity? Jan McGonigal, a game developer, reviewed the literature on this concept and found that building resilience—the ability to recover from difficulties—is the key. Ms. McGonigal's work led her to discover that there are four categories of resilience that can facilitate post-traumatic growth.[13] They are as follows:

- *Physical resilience*—strengthening yourself physically, being active, to help you better withstand stress (as was mentioned in a previous section on exercise)
- *Mental resilience*—changing your perspective about difficulties and adversity
- *Emotional resilience*—learning how to increase positive and decrease negative emotions
- *Social resilience*—developing strength through social relationships

As you make a deliberate effort to develop in each of these areas, you become better able to withstand difficulties and will actually grow to be a more effective individual in your home, workplace, and society in general.

This principle of growing from adversity is also one that is emphasized by several Bible writers. In fact, many of these authors encourage us to look on our difficulties with joy because of what they can teach us. (For more on what true joy is, please read the chapter on cultivating happiness). For example, in Romans 5:3, Paul states: "But we glory in tribulations also: knowing that tribulation worketh patience." And in James 1:2, 3 we are told: "My brethren, count it all joy when ye fall into divers temptations; knowing this, that the trying of your faith worketh patience." When we grasp and accept the idea that growth can come from adversity, it is then that we can understand and experience the true joy that is described by these and other Bible writers.

I would also like to emphasize two virtues or character strengths (as titled by experts in positive psychology) that are especially important for the experience of growth after adversity or trauma—forgiveness and gratitude. Regarding gratitude, the Bible tells us "In every thing give thanks" (1 Thessalonians 5:18). This is a principle that is beneficial not only spiritually but, mentally and emotionally as well. Dr. Robert Emmons, an expert on the topic of gratitude, states that when we express gratitude we block negative emotions, and experience higher levels of positive emotions, more joy and pleasure in life, greater stress resilience, and more optimism and happiness.[14] And, all of this contributes to optimal mental health.

It is also important to note that the previously mentioned Bible verse indicates that "in every thing" we should be thankful. Even when we experience adversity, we can find something for which we can be grateful. Dr. Emmons tells us that a grateful attitude in trials can energize, heal, and bring hope in the midst of our difficulties. It can also help us not to take things for granted.[15]

Forgiveness, on the other hand, involves making the choice to show mercy towards those who have hurt us. When we choose to forgive, we make an intentional decision to let go of the offense instead of seeking revenge or punishment. We may not instantly experience positive feelings toward those who mistreat us at the time that we decide to forgive. But, when we make that conscious choice to extend mercy to those who have wronged us, the process of healing begins. We are released from the "prison" of our bitterness, anger, and resentment, which helps us grow from our adversity.

There are several verses in the Bible in which the writers admonish us to forgive (see Ephesians 4:32; Mark 11:25; Colossians 3:13). In fact, when Peter asked how many times we should forgive those who hurt us, he was told by Jesus that he should forgive them "seventy times seven." This command to forgive was primarily given to us for our spiritual growth and development. However, when we choose to practice this principle we also reap the results of optimum wellness, which includes mental health.

An example of the power of forgiveness is illustrated by my work with one of my clients. This woman had been sexually assaulted by a number of men in her childhood (and adulthood). She had seen many counselors for this, but continued to struggle with the pain of being abused. As we talked, I presented to her the concept of forgiveness as it relates to healing. Slowly, she began to work on forgiving those who had hurt her. It was a gradual process, but at the end of our time together she indicated that she had made much progress in healing. And she attributed this to making the decision to release her feelings of anger and bitterness to those who had offended her.

So, it is possible that adversity can make us stronger. However, we must be ever careful to show patience and compassion to those who have experienced traumatic and painful life experiences. If you are currently dealing with adversity in your life—past or present—it is important to persevere and consistently do what you can to become stronger. The experience of growth after trauma is a process that takes time, and even some pain and hardship. But, if you endure, this growth will make you stronger and will help you on the road to achieving optimal mental health!

PRACTICAL APPLICATION

1. Take a day or so to examine your life and see which of the four areas of resilience you may need to develop. Make a commitment to work on one area at a time per week or per month.
2. Think of one or two difficult times in your life. After contemplating it for a while, write down what you have learned from those experiences. If possible, also indicate how you believe you have grown or developed as a person.
3. At the end of each day, write down three things for which you are grateful. You may also consider keeping a gratitude journal and writing in it on a weekly basis.
4. Think about your life and determine if you are harboring any resentment or bitterness towards anyone or anything in your life, past

or present. Make the decision to let go of these feelings and forgive. You may not immediately "feel" any different, but as you continue to stick to this decision, you will find that you will experience more peace and joy over time.

CHAPTER 5

DEVELOP A HEALTHY CONSCIENCE

I ONCE READ a story about a pilot who ignored the computerized voice from the automatic warning system of the plane telling him to "pull up, pull up." The pilot obviously thought the system was malfunctioning and turned it off. A few minutes later, the plane crashed into the side of the mountain and 191 people were killed! The automatic warning system voice on this plane is similar to that "voice" that we hear inside our heads telling us what is right or wrong. This is the *conscience*—and we all were created with this faculty of the mind. But, as was the case with the pilot in the story, we often ignore (or violate) the instruction given to us by that voice and the results are disastrous. However, if we can learn to listen to and follow our conscience, we will discover that this can help us in many ways, especially when it comes to our mental health. Let's explore this in more detail.

How does the conscience work? There are three general functions of the conscience. They are follows:

- *Points us to what to do*—tells us what to think, say, do in various situations
- *Judges our actions, thoughts, attitudes*—after we think, do or say something, the conscience evaluates it based on what we know is right or wrong
- *Passes sentence*—this occurs when we experience guilt or shame if we've violated the conscience (or the absence of these emotions if it is determined we did not violate it)

As we consider how the conscience functions, we can see that our response to its "voice" can impact our mental state. If the conscience is violated, we will experience feelings of guilt and shame. Eventually, this can lead to problems with various psychological concerns, such as depression. However, when we make a decision to heed the voice of conscience, we can reap great benefits. For example, there was a story of a woman who struggled with depression. One day after learning about the influence of the conscience on mental well-being, she decided to pay special attention to follow what she knew to be right, such as not talking about her friends, not taking home items at work that did not belong to her, and other things. As she did this, guess what happened? Yes, her depression eventually went away and she experienced a sense of peace that she had not known for a long time.

Some individuals persistently ignore their conscience. When this happens, they can eventually become desensitized to that voice and what seemed so "terrible" before becomes more tolerable over time. Some believe this is what happens when people commit horrendous crimes of violence that we often hear about in the news.

However, not everyone who persistently disregards the voice of conscience ends up engaging in openly horrific acts. Some end up becoming less sensitive to wrongdoing and may develop a conscience that is "seared with a hot iron" as referred to by the Bible writer Paul in 1 Timothy 4:2. When a body part is scorched or burned with a hot iron, that part of the body loses the ability to feel anything. So, it is with the conscience of these persons. It becomes insensitive to wrongdoing and guilt. These persons also have a more difficult time recognizing their unhealthy behavior, which makes it hard for them to feel a need to change. In addition, they tend to lose their sense of compassion, empathy, and sensitivity, which can impair their relationships with others.

So, it is important that we listen to that "voice" of conscience. However, in order for our conscience to adequately guide us, it must be sufficiently educated. If we are given inaccurate information about what is right and wrong from various sources—including our families, media, friends, and books—we will not be able to trust that "voice." For example, we can be taught that violence is an appropriate method for dealing with conflict. This can be learned through exposure to violent media (TV or movies) or growing up in a home where family members were violent toward each other. These experiences may educate that "voice" of conscience to tell us that violence—verbal or physical—is appropriate in our interactions with others. But, as we are told in Proverbs 16:25, "There is a way that seemeth right unto a man, but the end thereof are the ways of death." If we listen to that voice and resort to violence in our relationships, the results are usually quite devastating.

On the opposite end, our conscience can be falsely trained by our parents (or others) to believe that certain attitudes or actions are wrong, when actually this is not the case. Such training can lead us to experience guilt when it is not appropriate. For example, some may have been taught that it is wrong for them to get something free from others or that it is wrong to spend money on self. In such situations, the consciences of these people may condemn them if they purchase something nice for themselves or if a person gives them a gift.

Thus, it is important that we expose ourselves to people and information that will teach us healthy morals and standards. I must add that for those who believe in God, the Bible is viewed as the most important resource for developing a healthy conscience. The principles in the Bible provide us with insight into what is right and wrong and can also be used as a barometer for whatever we may learn from other sources, such as from society, media, etc.

To some, the contents of this chapter may seem loaded with moralistic overtones. However, I decided to risk this reaction from some readers. Why? Because in my work as a psychologist, I have met many who suffer from guilt, shame, and unhappiness due to not understanding the influence of conscience on their mental well-being. It is my strong belief that when we develop the habit of educating our conscience with healthy stimuli and listening to its "voice," we will reap the reward of a healthy, strong mind, which is essential for optimal mental health.

PRACTICAL APPLICATION

1. Take some time to write down what you consider to be important "rules" by which you should live. For example, it may be important for you to be a responsible citizen, an honest person, a compassionate friend, etc.
2. Try to pay more attention to your conscience as it directs you as to what is right or wrong. Make a concerted effort to follow your conscience.
3. Evaluate what you read, listen to, and watch and see if you are gaining healthy or unhealthy guidelines for your life. Make changes that will help your conscience to be accurately trained in order that you can be guided correctly.
4. If you are suffering with guilt and shame for past conscience violations and have not successfully resolved these emotions, I would like to suggest that you consider

dealing with them from a spiritual perspective. If you are not a religious person, it would be helpful if you looked for resources and/or people who can help you in this area (this may also be helpful even if you are religious).

CHAPTER 6

FOCUS LESS ON SELF AND MORE ON OTHERS

We live in a world that encourages us to focus on "me, myself, and I." We are taught to gratify self, esteem self, and do whatever we can to make ourselves feel good. Some mental health experts believe that this intense focus on self has not turned out for the best. For example:

> In trying to build a society that celebrates high self-esteem, self-expression, and 'loving yourself,' Americans have inadvertently created more narcissists—and a culture that brings out the narcissistic behavior in all of us. (The self-esteem fad apparently has backfired, but the folks at your local public or parochial grade school don't seem to have noticed).[16]

Other mental health experts disagree with this view and question the idea that the self-esteem movement has made us more self-centered. However, from my perspective, an increased self-focus *is* a significant problem in the lives of many people and in order to achieve optimal mental health, this has to change.

I believe that one of the most helpful methods for directing focus away from self is to purposefully become more focused on others—specifically, helping and giving to those who are in need. It has been found that those who show a selfless concern for the well-being of others (known as "altruism") tend to have better mental health.[17] There is also evidence that altruism and kindness to others is connected to better life satisfaction and more rewarding relationships, both of which are related to mental health.

Actually, this principle is not a new concept at all. Consider the following Bible verse:

> Is not this the fast that I have chosen? to loose the bands of wickedness, to undo the heavy burdens, and to let the oppressed go free, and that ye break every yoke? Is it not to deal thy bread to the hungry, and that thou bring the poor that are cast out to thy house? when

thou seest the naked, that thou cover him; and that thou hide not thyself from thine own flesh? **Then shall thy light break forth as the morning, and thine health shall spring forth speedily** [Isaiah 58:6-8, emphasis supplied].

Here we see that when we address the apparent needs of others—hunger, homelessness, poverty, etc.—our health (which includes mental health) "spring(s) forth speedily" or improves. However, in addition to these more obvious acts of kindness, we can also decrease our self-centeredness in other ways. This includes being kinder and less selfish with those who are close to us such as spouses, children, coworkers, and neighbors. We can also practice denying self, such as choosing not to take the larger portion of a dish at a meal, deciding not to buy a piece of clothing that we really want but really don't need, or letting someone with less groceries go ahead of you in a line at the supermarket (even if you're in a hurry). The list is endless on what we can do to become less self-focused.

The conclusion is this: If we want to enhance our mental health, it is important that we become less self-centered and more other-centered. But there is a caution to be added here. We must not seek to help or be kind to others merely for the benefits that come to us, which includes improved health. Our motives for helping others must be constantly examined. That is why Paul says in 1 Corinthians 13:3, "And though I bestow all my goods to feed the poor, and though I give my body to be burned, and have not charity [love], it profiteth me nothing." We don't want to defeat the purpose of not being self-centered by only doing good for others because of what we can gain. When we help others, we should be motivated by compassion, empathy, and even love. Our acts of kindness must be based on a selfless concern for their needs. It is then that we will experience true optimal mental health.

PRACTICAL APPLICATION:

1. Monitor your life for a couple of days and note how much time you spend thinking about and focusing on your needs versus the needs of others.
2. Make an effort to engage in various acts of kindness with strangers for a day or two. Observe how this impacts your life on those particular days.
3. If you are not already involved in volunteer work, determine if you can contribute a

couple of hours a week volunteering in your church, school, and/or community.
4. Work on being more helpful and less self-centered right in your own home and with your own family. You will be amazed at the impact this may have!

CHAPTER 7

CULTIVATE LASTING HAPPINESS

HAPPINESS—MOST VIEW IT as a state of feeling good. So, we spend time and effort looking for and engaging in pleasurable activities that will produce positive feelings. As we look around it is easy to see that this view of happiness is predominant in our society, our world. There are increasing efforts made to come up with some new gadget, activity, or experience that provides fun and excitement. This form of happiness is easily attained because there is no shortage of available and accessible pleasurable activities.

But happiness involves more than fun and pleasure. Experts in the field of positive psychology tell us that there are actually three dimensions of happiness:

1. Experiencing pleasure
2. Using our strengths and virtues to be engaged with others
3. Having a life with meaning and purpose[18]

Interestingly, the research suggests that those who obtain happiness through meaning and purpose experience the most life satisfaction. On the other hand, those who are focused mostly on experiencing pleasure report the least satisfaction with life.[19]

So, what else can we learn from mental health experts (based on scientific research) about lasting happiness that brings satisfaction? Significant work has been done in studying the lives of people who are genuinely happy. Researchers have discovered that these individuals have certain common habits. These habits are ones that can be adopted by most all of us. And, if we practice them, we too can experience true happiness. They include the following:

1. Using coping strategies that help one to handle difficulties more effectively, such as:
   - Finding the good in unfortunate situations
   - Not spending too much time thinking about problems
   - Accepting situations that cannot be changed
2. Improving the ability to recover quickly from difficulties, which is also called resilience
3. Building and maintaining quality relationships with others by expressing gratitude,

helping and doing nice things for others, cultivating compassion, etc.
4. Finding meaning and purpose in life.[20]

The Bible also reveals principles that are associated with happiness. For example, in Matthew 5:3-12 (better known as the Beatitudes) Jesus declares that those who have certain character traits and attitudes are "blessed" or happy. These include, but are not limited to: exhibiting mercy or compassion, having pure motives, demonstrating a meek spirit, pursuing peace, and even being mistreated for doing what is right. The wise man Solomon in Proverbs 3:13 also says that we can obtain happiness when we find wisdom.

The information presented from both science and the Bible reveals that happiness is more than just feeling good or experiencing pleasure. In fact, there may be experiences related to true happiness that are actually unpleasant and may involve a great amount of personal hardship and effort.[21] For example, it takes effort and courage to develop some of the character traits mentioned by Jesus (in the Beatitudes) that lead to happiness. Also, many of the habits of genuinely happy people, such as finding the good in unfortunate situations or maintaining quality relationships, takes work and is not easily developed. In the short term, these practices may not *feel* good. But over the long haul, they yield a sense of contentment and joy that is enduring and stable—in other words, a lasting happiness.

Suffice it to say that happiness is something that can be attained by everyone, no matter the life circumstances or situations. As one author states, "Each one possesses in himself [herself] the source of his [her] own happiness or wretchedness."[22] We have the ability to experience true, lasting happiness. The idea is not to merely pursue feeling happy, but to do that which engages us in life and provides meaning and purpose. When this is pursued, we will reap the rewards, which include the achieving of optimal mental health.

PRACTICAL APPLICATION:

1. How much time and effort do you put towards pursuing happy feelings? Are you easily bored? Take some time to determine how much you depend on activities, events, or people that you believe bring fun or excitement in your life. Based on what was shared

in this chapter, what changes do you need to make in how you pursue happiness?
2. What brings purpose and meaning to your life? Is it your job, your family, your romantic relationship, your children, or any material possessions? Take some time to think about this and determine if you need to readjust your focus and develop different priorities in your life.
3. Review the Beatitudes in Matthew 5:3-12 and the habits of happy people. Determine which of these practices are ones that you need to incorporate in your life. Start to make some changes today!

CHAPTER 8

DEVELOP AN ACTIVE RELIGIOUS LIFE

When I was training to become a psychologist over 20 years ago, religion was a topic that was shunned by many professionals in this discipline. Oftentimes this was because religion—defined as belief and worship of a superhuman controlling power—was viewed in a negative light, especially as it related to mental health. However, there is now increasing evidence that religion can have a positive effect on mental well-being. For example, it has been found that individuals who view religion or spirituality as important in their lives have a significantly lower risk of experiencing major depression compared with those who do not.[23] It has also been found that religious people tend to cope more effectively with stressful life events and have better mental health than nonreligious people.[24,25]

When one refers to religion, this can include many different faiths, such as Christianity, Buddhism, Hinduism, and Judaism. However, the religion that will be highlighted here is Christianity. A very important aspect of the Christian religion is faith, which involves belief, trust, confidence, and reassurance. Christians who are active with their belief and practices put their faith in God. When faith is exercised in God, it leads to the recognition that there is a power/person who exists outside of self, which helps us to accept our limits as human beings. We also learn to release control in areas that are beyond our human control. This can help to reduce stress, relieve anxiety, and provide a sense of peace.

The exercising of trust and belief in God also provides a keener awareness of the meaning and purpose of our individual lives. In addition, it can provide strength to do whatever needs to be done to obtain mental well-being, which can include help for applying many of the principles cited in this book!

Another important aspect of the Christian religion is the belief that the Bible, God's Word, provides important guidelines for everyday, practical living (which also involves faith). There are many principles in the Bible that can help our minds to function more effectively. Those who are active in the Christian faith believe that if they practice these principles, it will have a positive influence in their lives, including their mental health.

Here are just a few examples of Bible texts that reveal such principles:

"A merry heart doeth good like a medicine: but a broken spirit drieth the bones" (Proverbs 17:22).

"For as he thinketh in his heart, so is he." (Proverbs 23:7).

"Take therefore no thought for the morrow: for the morrow shall take thought for the things of itself. Sufficient unto the day is the evil thereof" (Matthew 6:34).

"For God hath not given us the spirit of fear; but of power, and of love, and of a sound mind" (2 Timothy 1:7).

"Finally, brethren, whatsoever things are true, whatsoever things are honest, whatsoever things are just, whatsoever things are pure, whatsoever things are lovely, whatsoever things are of good report; if there be any virtue, and if there be any praise, think on these things" (Philippians 4:8).

In my work as a psychologist, I have often utilized the principles from the Bible to help others enhance their mental functioning. For example, in dealing with anxiety or worry, I have encouraged individuals to take one day at a time and not become too preoccupied with future worries (based on Matthew 6:34). Or, to help develop healthy thinking patterns, I have recommended memorizing verses such as Philippians 4:8. Whether or not one has specific emotional/mental concerns, the principles from the Bible can help strengthen the mind and enhance mental well-being.

The final component of Christianity that will be considered is the principle of love, which is a foundational piece of the Christian faith. Christians believe that God loves them and that He exhibits this love in many ways. What is the significance of this understanding when it comes to mental health? Consider the following quote by a psychiatrist:

> I've seen non-spiritual folk struggle more, perhaps, with feeling they are unloved and unworthy when traumatized than those with a spiritual 'back-up' who feel that, no matter what happens, they have a spiritual connection to something greater. In addition, the

> spiritual and religious don't seem to wrestle as much with those existential questions of 'Why am I here? What is my purpose?' that can plague the non-spiritual.[26]

It is amazing that this observation was made by a mental health professional who does not claim to be a Christian or even religious! Even though it is not based on any scientific research, per se, I believe the statement was noteworthy of mention because it provides another perspective on how religion can be beneficial for optimal mental health.

It is also important to recognize that for Christians the love that comes from God is often reciprocated in the love that they show not only to God but, to their fellow human beings. The benefits from demonstrating this love include increased faith in God as well as increased selflessness in our interactions with others, as was discussed in a previous chapter.

Now, I must say that not all religious people fare better with their mental health. Some individuals may experience more mental/emotional difficulties based on their beliefs. For example, it has been found that people who believe in an angry, vengeful God are more likely to suffer from social anxiety, paranoia, obsessional thinking, and compulsions.[27] Therefore, it seems important that for religion to contribute to optimal mental health, it is essential to have beliefs and practices that accurately represent who God is—a loving, compassionate, yet firm and powerful being. As a Christian, this can only be obtained from a clear understanding of His Word, the Bible.

So, what can we conclude about religion and mental health? Based on what has been shared in this chapter, it appears that when our religious life involves an active faith in God, a life based on principles from the Bible, a belief that God loves us and that we can respond with love to Him (and each other), as well as a correct understanding of who God is, we can be well on our way to achieving even more optimal mental health and well-being.

PRACTICAL APPLICATION

1. Take some time to look at your life and see what you may do to enhance your spiritual life. This may include daily Bible reading, spending more time in prayer, and/or reading other inspired religious books.

2. Spend time asking God for strength to implement the principles revealed in this book. He can give us the motivation and the power to follow through with what we need to do to experience optimal mental health.
3. If interested, find someone who can help you with your spiritual concerns. This may include a person who you know is spiritually grounded or a pastor. Also, if you are not connected with a church, strongly consider finding one. It is amazing how attending and being involved in the right church can contribute to spiritual growth!

CHAPTER 9

A BRIEF SUMMARY

As you can see from what has been shared in this book, it is quite possible to experience optimal mental health. However, this is not something that occurs overnight. As with anything that is beneficial for us, it takes time and patience to develop. You must be active in pursuing this and be willing, at times, to struggle through some painstaking effort to achieve the desired results.

As a brief review, a summary of the "keys" to optimal mental health include:

- Living a healthy lifestyle (diet, exercise, sleep, etc.)
- Changing our thought patterns
- Practicing self-control in all areas of our lives
- Learning to grow from our adversity
- Developing a healthy, educated conscience
- Focusing less on self and more on others

- Cultivating happiness that will last
- Developing an active religious life

If these principles are pursued on a consistent, regular basis, the results will be amazing! I challenge you today to make a decision to follow these steps. You will be glad that you did!

ENDNOTES

1. Walsh, R., "Lifestyle and Mental Health," *American Psychologist*, 6 (7), pp. 579-592 (2011).

2. White, E., *Mind, Character, and Personality*, vol. 1, p. 235. Nashville, TN: Southern Publishing Association, 1977.

3. Peet, M., "International variations in the outcome of schizophrenia and the prevalence of depression in relation to national dietary practices: an ecological analysis," *British Journal of Psychiatry*, 184, pp. 404-408 (2004).

4. Chepulis, L. M., et al, "The effects of long-term honey, sucrose or sugar-free diets on memory and anxiety in rats," *Physiology & Behavior*, 97 (3-4), pp. 359-368 (2009).

5. Mattson, M. P., et al, "Meal frequency and timing in health and disease," *Proceedings of the National Academy of Sciences of the United States of America*, 111 (47) 16647-53 (2014).

6. White, E. G., *Counsels on Diet and Foods*, p. 181. Washington, DC: Review & Herald Publishing Association, 1976.

7. Peri, C., "What lack of sleep does to your mind." Retrieved from http:/webmd.com, 2010.

8. White, E., *Manuscript Releases*, No. 7, p. 224. Washington, DC: Review & Herald Publishing Association, 1990.

9. Bowler, D. E.; Buyung-Ali, L. M.; Knight, T. M.; and Pullin, A. S., "A systematic review of evidence for the added benefits to health of exposure to natural environments," *BMC Public Health*, *10* (10), p. 456 (2010).

10. White, E. G., *In Heavenly Places*, p. 164, Washington, DC: Review & Herald Publishing Association, 1967.

11. Nedley, Neil, *Depression Recovery Program Manual*, Ardmore, OK: Nedley Publishing Company, 2005.

12. Adapted from Baumeister, R. and Tierney. J., *Willpower: Rediscovering the greatest human strength*, New York: Penguin Publishing Group, 2011.

13. McGonigal, J., "The game that can give you 10 extra years of life." Retrieved from https://www.ted.com/talks/jane_mcgonigal_the_game_that_can_give_you_10_extra_years_of_life?language=en (2012, June).

14. Robert Emmons. Retrieved from http://greater-good.berkeley.edu/article/item/why_gratitude_is_good (November 6, 2010).

15. Robert Emmons. Retrieved from http://greater-good.berkeley.edu/article/item/how_gratitude_can_help_you_through_hard_times (May 10, 2013).

16. Twenge, J. and Campbell, K., *The Narcissism Epidemic*, New York, New York: Atria Paperback, 2009.

17. Schwarz, C.; Meisenhelder, J. B.; Ma Y.; Reed, G., "Altruistic social interest behaviors are associated with better mental health," *Psychosomatic Medicine*, 65(5), 778-85 (2003).

18. Seligman, Martin. Retrieved from http://www.ted.com/talks/martin_seligman_on_the_state_of_psychology?language=en#t-915451 (February 2004).

19. *Ibid.*

20. Kurtz, Jamie, seminar, lecture on "Habits of Happy People, 2015.

21. Grenville-Cleave, Bridget, *Positive psychology: A practical guide*, London, England: Icon Books, 2012.

22. White, E. G., *Mind, Character, and Personality*, vol. 2, p. 642, Hagerstown, MD; Review & Herald Publishing Association, 1977.

23. Miller, L., et al., "Religiosity and Major Depression in Adults at High Risk: A ten-year prospective study," *American Journal of Psychiatry*, 169 (1) pp. 89-94 (2012).

24. Koenig, H., "Research on Religion, Spirituality, and Mental Health: A review," *Canadian Journal of Psychiatry*, 54 (5) pp. 283-291 (2009).

25. Johnstone, Brick, et al., "Relationships Among Spirituality, Religious Practices, Personality Factors, and Health for Five Different Faiths," *Journal of Religion and Health*, 1 (4), pp. 76-80, doi10.1007/s10943-012-9615 (2012).

26. Deans, Emily, M.D. "Brains, Spirituality, and Depression: Does being religious protect the brain from depression?" Retrieved from https://

www.psychologytoday.com/blog/evolutionary-psychiatry/201401/brains-spirituality-and-depression (January 2014).

27. Silton, N., et al., "Beliefs About God and Mental Health Among American Adults," *Journal of Religion and Health*, 53 (5), pp. 1285-1296 (2014)..

Made in the USA
Columbia, SC
19 July 2018